Frida Kahlo

Jill A. Laidlaw

FRANKLIN WATTS
LONDON•SYDNEY

First published in 2003 by
Franklin Watts
96 Leonard Street,
London EC2A 4XD

Franklin Watts Australia
45-51 Huntley Street,
Alexandria,
NSW 2015

Series Editor: Adrian Cole
Editor: Mary-Jane Wilkins
Series Designer: Mo Choy
Art Director: Jonathan Hair
Picture Researcher: Julie McMahon

A CIP catalogue record for this book
is available from the British Library.

ISBN 0 7496 4658 6

Printed in Hong Kong, China

Acknowledgements

AKG, London: cover bottom left & p7b; p10b; cover bc & p11t; p15 Portrait of Miguel N. Lira, 1927 © (2003) Banco de México Diego Rivera & Frida Kahlo Museums Trust. Av. Cinco de Mayo No. 2, Col. Centro, Del. Cuauhtémoc 06059, México, D.F; p16t Tina Modotti 1929; p20t Edward Weston 1930; p24t; cover br & p38t. Art Archive: p9b The Blue House, Coyoacan / Nicolas Sapieha; p31 The Two Fridas, 1939 / Museum of Modern Art, Mexico / Dagli Orti / © (2003) Banco de México Diego Rivera & Frida Kahlo Museums Trust. Av. Cinco de Mayo No. 2, Col. Centro, Del. Cuauhtémoc 06059, México, D.F.; p36b Bedroom of Frida Kahlo; p41b. Art Resource, NY: p37 Self Portrait with Monkey, 1945 / Museum Robert Brady, Cuernavaca, Mexico / © (2003) Banco de México Diego Rivera & Frida Kahlo Museums Trust. Av. Cinco de Mayo No. 2, Col. Centro, Del. Cuauhtémoc 06059, México, D.F. Artothek: p28t Museum of Modern Art, New York: © Salvador Dali, Gala-Salvador Dali Foundation, DACS, London 2003. Biblioteca des las Artes / Banco de México: p6; p7t; p8t; p8b; p9t; p16b; p18; p38b; p41t – all photographs © (2003) Banco de México Diego Rivera & Frida Kahlo Museums Trust. Av. Cinco de Mayo No. 2, Col. Centro, Del. Cuauhtémoc 06059, México, D.F. Biblioteca des las Artes / Banco de Mexico: artworks: p12 Accident, 1926 (sketch) © (2003) Banco de México Diego Rivera & Frida Kahlo Museums Trust. Av. Cinco de Mayo No. 2, Col. Centro, Del. Cuauhtémoc 06059, México, D.F; p13 Self portrait in a Velvet Dress, 1926 © (2003) Banco de México Diego Rivera & Frida Kahlo Museums Trust. Av. Cinco de Mayo No. 2, Col. Centro, Del. Cuauhtémoc 06059, México, D.F; p17 Frida and Diego Rivera, 1931 © (2003) Banco de México Diego Rivera & Frida Kahlo Museums Trust. Av. Cinco de Mayo No. 2, Col. Centro, Del. Cuauhtémoc 06059, México, D.F p33 Self Portrait with Braid, 1941 © (2003) Banco de México Diego Rivera & Frida Kahlo Museums Trust. Av. Cinco de Mayo No. 2, Col. Centro, Del. Cuauhtémoc 06059, México, D.F; p35 The Bride Frightened at Seeing Life Opened, 1943 © (2003) Banco de México Diego Rivera & Frida Kahlo Museums Trust. Av. Cinco de Mayo No. 2, Col. Centro, Del. Cuauhtémoc 06059, México, D.F; p39 Marxism Will Give Health to the Sick, 1954 © (2003) Banco de México Diego Rivera & Frida Kahlo Museums Trust. Av. Cinco de Mayo No. 2, Col. Centro, Del. Cuauhtémoc 06059, México, D.F.; p40 © (2003) Banco de México Diego Rivera & Frida Kahlo Museums Trust. Av. Cinco de Mayo No. 2, Col. Centro, Del. Cuauhtémoc 06059, México, D.F. Bridgeman: p22b / Library of National Congress, Washington D.C., USA; p25b / Illustrated London News Picture Library; Centre Pompidou-MNAM-CCI, Paris / RMN p29 Self Portrait The Frame, 1938. Christie's Images, Ltd: p23 My Dress Hangs There or New York, 1933 © (2003) Banco de México Diego Rivera & Frida Kahlo Museums Trust. Av. Cinco de Mayo No. 2, Col. Centro, Del. Cuauhtémoc 06059, México, D.F. Corbis: cover, main picture & p21 Self-Portrait on the Borderline Between Mexico and the United States, 1932 / Christie's Images © (2003) Banco de México Diego Rivera & Frida Kahlo Museums Trust. Av. Cinco de Mayo No. 2, Col. Centro, Del. Cuauhtémoc 06059, México, D.F p27 Memory or The Heart, 1937 © (2003) Banco de México Diego Rivera & Frida Kahlo Museums Trust. Av. Cinco de Mayo No. 2, Col. Centro, Del. Cuauhtémoc 06059, México, D.F; p28b / Stefano Bianchetti; p32 / Bettmann; p43. Culver Pictures: p22t. Hulton: p30b / Archive Photos; p34t / Archive Photos; p36t / Archive Photos. Magnum Photos: p24b / Marilyn Silverstone. Mary Evans Picture Library: p10t. Popperfoto: p11b; p19b. South American Pictures: p14; p19t; p26t / Tony Morrison; p26b / Iain Pearson. Topham Picturepoint: p20b; p25t; p34b. Werner Forman Archive: p30t / British Museum, London.

Whilst every attempt has been made to clear copyright
should there be any inadvertent omission please apply
in the first instance to the publisher regarding rectification.

Contents

Who was Frida Kahlo?

Frida Kahlo was a Mexican nationalist, a Communist, the wife of Diego Rivera (1886-1957), a witty friend, an inspiring teacher, and a woman determined to live a full life, no matter what happened to her. Above all, Frida Kahlo was a painter.

▲ Frida Kahlo aged 6, in a photograph taken by her father. Here Kahlo is happy and smiling, something which she doesn't often have a reason to do in her later portraits.

A LIFE IN PAINT

Kahlo painted portraits, still lifes, landscapes and self-portraits. During her lifetime she created about 200 paintings. Most of them are comparatively small in size (they average only 30 x 37 cm) and this makes them seem even more personal, as though they were never meant for public display. Just over half of them are self-portraits which she painted as a way of recording the passing events in her life.

> *'I will write to you with my eyes...'*
>
> *Frida Kahlo*

KAHLO'S WORLD

Kahlo's paintings, with their deeply personal meanings and often revealing symbols and imagery, invite us into her world – which was often a sad, lonely or painful one. She created many of her paintings in an attempt to make sense of these feelings. In her self-portraits it is impossible to look at her mask-like face or into her eyes without sharing something of her experience.

WOMEN ARTISTS

At the beginning of the twentieth century there were few successful women artists in Europe and the Americas. There were many reasons for this, but prejudice was the main one. Art was viewed as a man's profession (as were most jobs).

There were also practical obstacles to women becoming artists. Women were unable to go to many art schools because people thought that art was an unsuitable subject for a woman to study – mainly because most art courses included drawing nude men.

At the time of Frida Kahlo's birth in 1907 it was very difficult for female artists to be taken seriously in a Catholic country such as Mexico. Kahlo blazed a trail for the women artists who followed her because she struggled against the odds to have her work exhibited and reviewed.

EARLY LIFE

Magdalena Carmen Frida Kahlo y Calderón was born on 6 July 1907 in Coyoacán, a suburb of Mexico City, to Matilde Calderón y González and Guillermo Kahlo. She was the third of four daughters.

Kahlo's father, Guillermo, was a German national who had emigrated to Mexico in 1891 at the age of 19. Guillermo's parents were Hungarian Jews and Frida's mother was descended from Indian and Spanish blood.

Frida Kahlo was a truly international child and a product of the melting pot of Mexican society.

▶ Matilde Calderón and Guillermo Kahlo on their wedding day in February 1898.

▲ Mexico City, c.1915. Today Mexico City is the world's largest city, but during Kahlo's childhood it was a much smaller place with a population of less than half a million people. It was full of contrasting streets of grand architecture (above) and extreme poverty.

Guillermo Kahlo was a successful architectural photographer and an amateur artist. He often took Kahlo with him when he went to paint in the countryside.

Eventually he saved enough money to buy a plot of land in Coyoacán. Here he built a large house for his growing family, called the Blue House (because it was painted a striking cobalt blue).

Childhood years

◀ A family portrait taken in 1913. Kahlo is standing on the far left and her sister Cristina sits with her legs crossed on the balcony wall. Their mother is standing on the balcony, second from the right.

▼ A self-portrait by Guillermo Kahlo c.1907. He was closer to Frida than to any of his other children.

In 1904 Guillermo Kahlo had been commissioned to photograph the country's most important pre-Columbian and colonial architectural sites by the ruler of Mexico, Porfirio Díaz (1830-1915). But in 1910 the Mexican Revolution (see pages 10-11) put an end to the rule of Díaz and Guillermo was suddenly out of a job. After that, work was hard to come by and the family struggled to make ends meet.

'It was with great difficulty that a livelihood was earned in my house.'

Frida Kahlo

TIMELINE ▶

1907	1910	1913	1920
Frida Kahlo is born on 6 July.	The Mexican Revolution begins.	Kahlo catches polio which leaves her lower right leg and foot deformed.	The Mexican Revolution ends.

▲ Kahlo in 1923, in her second year as a pupil at the National Preparatory School.

GOING TO SCHOOL

Despite the fact that Kahlo missed a lot of her early education through illness (see panel), she did very well at school. She had a photographic memory and only had to read a book once to remember everything in it. She found it easy to learn languages, and could read and speak English, Spanish and German. Kahlo's interests were wide-ranging and she loved the sciences as well as art and literature. After primary school she went to the Escuela Nacional Preparatoria (the National Preparatory School), the best secondary school in Mexico. Here she was one of only 35 girls among 2,000 boys. Kahlo decided to become a doctor.

EARLY ILLNESS

At the age of six Kahlo caught polio, a disease which affects the brain and spine and can lead to partial or total paralysis (loss of movement).

Kahlo survived polio but her recovery was long and difficult and she had to stay in her room at the Blue House for nine months. Her right leg became thin and withered as a result of the illness. Guillermo encouraged his daughter to exercise her leg by playing football, boxing, swimming and wrestling – sports not played by girls at this time in Mexico.

Kahlo disguised her thin leg and foot by wearing three or four pairs of socks and a shoe with a built-up heel and sole. Later in life she wore men's suits or flamboyant peasant costumes with long skirts which covered her legs.

▲ The Blue House in Coyoacán. When she was ill Kahlo spent much of her time at the family home.

Revolutionary Mexico

In 1910, Mexico was plunged into a revolution after 34 years of rule by the dictator Porfirio Díaz. The revolution resulted in a civil war which lasted ten years.

Frida Kahlo identified with the revolutionary cause to such an extent that throughout her life she lied about the year of her birth, saying that it was 1910, rather than 1907. Kahlo wanted to make the point that she considered herself reborn when the 'true' Mexico began to take shape.

▲ Porfirio Díaz, Mexico's powerful ruler, studied to be a priest, but joined the army when war broke out between Mexico and the USA in 1846.

A TROUBLED PAST

Mexico had been ruled by a series of ancient and sophisticated civilisations, including the Toltecs, the Mayans and the Aztecs. The Aztecs controlled most of Mexico from AD 1200 and they were the country's rulers when the Spanish arrived in 1519.

The Spanish force was led by Hernán Cortés (1485-1547), a violent and ruthless soldier and explorer, who had been sent by the Spanish monarchy to conquer Mexico. By 1521 Cortés had completed the conquest. For the next three centuries Mexico was ruled mainly by the Spanish.

Mexico gained independence from Spain in 1810, but it was a poor country. Other countries, including the USA and Great Britain, used it as a source of cheap labour and natural resources, such as oil. Mexicans became tired of this foreign interference and also disliked the government of Porfirio Díaz, which was slow to make social changes.

▲ The Aztec emperor Montezuma II (left) greeting the Spanish explorer Hernán Cortés, shortly before Cortés killed 10,000 of Montezuma's people and took him prisoner.

▶ Revolutionary leader Francisco Madero and his supporters celebrate the defeat of Porfirio Díaz in June 1911. Madero was elected president later that year.

A TROUBLED FUTURE

The revolution of 1910 began with outbreaks of fighting. Different parts of the country fought under three main regional leaders: Pascual Orozco (1882-1915), Pancho Villa (1878-1923) and Emiliano Zapata (1879-1919). Francisco Madero (1873-1913), a revolutionary leader who had been defeated in elections by Díaz, was elected president in 1911. But he was betrayed and shot in 1913.

For the following eight years the revolutionary groups fought among themselves. Finally, in 1920, General Alvaro Obregón (1880-1928) led a bloodless revolution, called a coup, and formed a government.

CHANGING THE CONSTITUTION

In 1917, a revised Mexican constitution had been drawn up. This formed the basis for Obregón's government and the governments that followed it. The constitution aimed to give free education to all, to give land to those who had none, to spend money on farming, to take Mexico's natural resources into state ownership, to pay a minimum wage, to give workers the right to strike and to introduce welfare and health programmes.

THE NEW MEXICO

After the revolution there was a revival of national pride. Composers created symphonies using Mexican folk themes, authors wrote about Mexican characters, stories and settings, artists drew Mexican peasants in traditional costumes, and choreographers created ballets based on Mexican folk dances.

◀ During a Mexican celebration (or *fiesta*), people wore their best clothes, drank *pulque* (home-brewed alcohol) and danced and sang traditional songs called *corridos*.

The accident

On 17 September 1925, when Kahlo was 18, she was on her way home from school with her boyfriend, Alejandro Gómez Arias, when the bus they were travelling in was hit by a large tram. The bus crumpled like a tin can. Alejandro was thrown under the tram and Kahlo was impaled on the metal arm of a seat in the wreckage of the bus.

A passer-by put his knee on Kahlo's chest and pulled the metal from her body. It is said she screamed so loudly that she drowned out the sound of sirens as help arrived at the scene.

▲ *Accident*, 1926. This small sketch in pencil, drawn by Kahlo exactly one year after the accident, is the only picture she drew of the horrific events that happened on 17 September 1925.

> *'The arms of the seat went through me like a sword into a bull.'*
>
> Frida Kahlo

KAHLO'S INJURIES

As a result of the crash Kahlo's spine was broken in three places, her collarbone and third and fourth ribs were broken, her right leg was broken in 11 places, her right foot smashed, and her pelvis almost destroyed.

Kahlo was taken to hospital and operated on, although the doctors did not expect her to live. She did survive, but suffered constant pain and tiredness and had to stay in bed for a month where, she told Alejandro, '… death dances around my bed at night'.

BEGINNING PAINTING

During the year following her accident Kahlo returned frequently to the hospital. She had to stay in bed, and was forced to wear plaster corsets to help her injured back. During this time she began to paint.

Self-Portrait in a Velvet Dress (opposite) is Kahlo's first serious self-portrait. 'My mother asked a carpenter to make me an easel, if that's what you can call the special apparatus which could be fixed onto my bed, because the plaster cast didn't allow me to sit up.'

TIMELINE ▶

1922–25	17 September 1925	1925–26
Kahlo goes to the Escuela Nacional Preparatoria (the National Preparatory School). She meets the artist Diego Rivera when he paints a mural at her school.	Kahlo is seriously injured in a road accident.	While recovering from her injuries Kahlo begins painting .

Self-Portrait in a Velvet Dress, 1926

oil on canvas 79.7 x 60 cm Bequest of Alejandro Gómez Arias, Mexico City

This painting was a gift for Kahlo's boyfriend, Alejandro Gómez Arias, and was her first proper work as an artist. It was influenced by European portrait painting. Kahlo shows herself in a traditional pose, wearing European-style clothes. We can already see the elements that dominate many of Kahlo's self-portraits: her single eyebrow, her direct look at the viewer, her long neck and full lips.

Back to life

Two years after the accident Kahlo began to pick up the pieces of her old life. Although she never fully recovered her physical health and did not return to school, she did continue to paint. One of her most striking early portraits is of Miguel N. Lira (opposite), a friend from the National Preparatory School. Lira was a writer and a poet who became one of Mexico's foremost lawyers.

USING SYMBOLS

The images in the background of Miguel's portrait include different symbols. The harp-like musical instrument directly above Miguel's head is called a lyre. It represents his surname, Lira, which means lyre in Spanish. The angel, behind Miguel and to the left, is the Archangel Michael (Michael is the English form of Miguel).

THE PEAKED CAPS

At school Kahlo had been a member of a group of seven boys and two girls who called themselves the Cachuchas, or 'the peaked caps', after the caps they wore.

The Cachuchas were famous for their practical jokes – they let off firecrackers during lectures and once rode a donkey through the halls of the school. They were also famous for their intelligence – they sometimes criticised teachers they thought were boring or stupid and they campaigned for reforms within the school.

The leader of the Cachuchas was Kahlo's boyfriend Alejandro Gómez Arias. Miguel N. Lira was also a member of the group.

TIMELINE ▶

1926	Summer 1926	September 1926	Late 1927
Kahlo recovers in bed, either at home or in hospital, after her accident. She does not return to school.	Kahlo falls ill again with pains in her back.	Doctors discover that three vertebrae in Kahlo's spine are out of place. Kahlo has to stay in bed in a plaster corset for four months.	Kahlo is up and about once more.

Portrait of Miguel N. Lira, 1927

oil on canvas 99.2 x 67.5 cm Instituto Tlaxcalteca de Cultura, Mexico

Kahlo hated this portrait of Miguel N. Lira, who was one of her Cachuchas friends. She felt that Lira looked like a cardboard cut-out. Kahlo described the picture in a letter to her boyfriend, Alejandro Gómez Arias: 'I am simply painting a portrait of Lira, totally ugly. [...] It's so bad that I simply don't know how he can tell me he likes it.'

Marriage

▲ Tina Modotti took this photograph of a mother and her children washing pans and bathing in a river in Tehuantepec, southern Mexico. Modotti took many photographs showing poverty in everyday Mexican life.

TINA MODOTTI

Tina Modotti (1846-1942) was an American-born photographer who moved to Mexico from the United States. She specialised in taking documentary photographs which reflected the inequality in society. She chose to concentrate on domestic scenes, capturing people in their everyday environment. She also took many photographs of Frida Kahlo and Diego Rivera.

Modotti was a strong political activist and she introduced Kahlo to the Mexican Communist Party in 1927.

By 1927 Kahlo's Cachuchas friends had gone to university. They became involved in politics, joining a group of left-wing activists. Kahlo also cared about politics and in 1928 she joined the Mexican Communist Party. She began giving speeches and taking part in marches and meetings.

FRIDA MEETS DIEGO

Kahlo met other Communist artists, writers, photographers and intellectuals at the weekly 'salons' held by photographer Tina Modotti (see panel). There she met Diego Rivera, an enthusiastic Communist and Mexico's greatest living artist.

After their first meeting Rivera described Kahlo: 'She had a fine nervous body, topped by a delicate face. Her hair was long; dark and thick eyebrows set above her nose. They seemed like the wings of a blackbird, their black arches framing two extraordinary brown eyes.' Kahlo showed Rivera her paintings and he was impressed enough to encourage her to become a full-time artist. They began spending more and more time with each other and quickly fell in love.

Kahlo and Rivera seemed an unlikely couple. Kahlo was a frail, unknown 21-year-old and Rivera was huge and robust – and 20 years older than Kahlo.

▶ Rivera and Kahlo on their wedding day, at Coyoacán town hall. Rivera wore a suit and Kahlo an outfit borrowed from her parents' maid.

TIMELINE ▶

1928	21 August 1929	October 1929
Kahlo joins the Mexican Communist Party. She meets Diego Rivera again.	Rivera and Kahlo marry.	The New York Stock Exchange crashes. The Great Depression begins.

Frida and Diego Rivera, 1931

oil on canvas 100 x 79 cm San Francisco Museum of Modern Art

This wedding portrait was painted by Kahlo a few years after the event. Kahlo seems to float next to her huge husband, her tiny feet unable to keep her on the ground. It is not clear whether she is floating because she feels great joy or because she feels insignificant in comparison with the great man she has married.

Diego Rivera

Diego Rivera was already a legend by the time he married Frida Kahlo in 1929. He was as famous for his lifestyle as for his art. He seemed to be awake 24 hours a day, behaved wildly at parties and held controversial Communist views (see pages 24-25).

Rivera created vast murals (wall paintings) in Mexico's most important hospitals, schools, palaces and government buildings. These murals made him Mexico's most famous 20th-century painter and one of the most influential artists of his time.

▲ Rivera and Kahlo on a demonstration, 1 May 1929. Kahlo wears the shirt and tie of the Communist Party – she wears the same shirt in the mural opposite.

BEGINNINGS

Rivera was one of twin brothers born to Maria and Diego Barrientos in 1886 in Guanajuato, an old Mexican silver-mining town. When he was only 18 months old Diego's twin brother died.

Rivera performed brilliantly at school, but he enjoyed art the most. When he was only ten years old he began to take night classes in drawing at San Carlos Academy, Mexico's finest art school. In 1906, at the age of 20, he won a scholarship to travel to Europe to study.

Between 1907 and 1909 Rivera journeyed through Spain, France, Belgium, Holland and England, absorbing art and experimenting with different painting styles. He finally settled in Paris.

RETURN TO MEXICO

Like Kahlo, Rivera was affected by the Mexican Revolution. He returned to Mexico City in 1921, after the end of the revolution. He said: 'An artist with my revolutionary point of view could now find a place in Mexico – a place in which to work and grow.'

Rivera was right. The Minister of Education, José Vasconcelos (1882-1950),

'Almost as soon as my fat baby fingers could grasp a pencil, I was marking up walls, doors and furniture.'

Diego Rivera

The Arsenal, a mural painted by Rivera between 1923 and 1928. Kahlo is right in the centre of the picture, dressed as a member of the Communist Party. She is handing out guns to Mexicans so they can fight for their rights.

employed artists such as Rivera to paint Mexican history on the walls of the country's most important buildings. Vasconcelos wanted to enable people who could not read to learn the history of their country through pictures. This group of painters became known as the Muralist Movement.

THE RIVERA STYLE

After such a long time away from Mexico, Rivera found that he saw his country with fresh eyes. This inspired him to turn away from the European styles of painting he had studied and to paint in his own way. Rivera wanted to create a Mexican style that would glorify the history of his country and give its peasant peoples the status of heroes.

Rivera's murals are packed with people, objects and events which show his incredible imagination. He had a brilliant mind, as well as an artist's eye and a skilful pair of hands. The paintings also draw on his wide knowledge of Mexican pre-Columbian and colonial history, art and culture.

A WORKAHOLIC

Rivera regularly worked an amazing 18-hour day, seven days a week. He sometimes worked for 24 hours at a time. He did not shut himself away when he worked – people came in from the street to talk to him. When he worked in the United States people even bought tickets to watch him paint.

◀ Rivera was famous for being able to work on a scaffold for days at a time, sleeping and eating there too.

The USA

▲ Rivera and Kahlo in San Francisco in November 1930.

KAHLO'S PREGNANCIES

Kahlo wanted more than anything to have a child, but her damaged body was unable to support a pregnancy. After 1932 Kahlo revealed her grief at her childlessness in many of her self-portraits. In her final years she told a friend, 'I lost three children... Paintings substituted for all of this.'

In October 1929 Kahlo resigned from the Communist Party. She was protesting at Rivera's expulsion from the party for taking a commission from the (non-Communist) Mexican government. In order to escape the increasingly hostile political environment, Rivera accepted a series of commissions in the United States. In November 1930 Kahlo and Rivera left Mexico to go to San Francisco.

IMPRESSIONS OF AMERICA

Kahlo explored San Francisco on foot while Rivera painted murals. She wrote: 'The city and bay are overwhelming', and, 'What is especially fantastic is Chinatown'.

Rivera and Kahlo returned briefly to Mexico in 1931, before going to New York for a retrospective of Rivera's work at the Museum of Modern Art. In April 1932 they moved to Detroit, where Rivera painted a mural.

▲ A view of San Francisco across the Golden Gate, c.1928.

Kahlo crammed her impressions of America into *Self-Portrait on the Borderline Between Mexico and the United States* (opposite). On the Mexican side of the painting (left) the sun and the moon nourish the land and nurture the plants. On the American side of the painting (right) factory smoke and skyscrapers leave no room in the sky for the sun and the moon, and the ground is planted with machines.

TIMELINE ▶

October 1929	1930	June 1931	April 1932	July 1932	Autumn 1932
Rivera is expelled from the Communist Party. Kahlo resigns in protest.	Kahlo's first pregnancy is ended. Kahlo and Rivera move to San Francisco where Rivera paints murals.	Kahlo and Rivera make a short trip back to Mexico before going to New York for a retrospective of Rivera's work.	Kahlo and Rivera travel to New York and Detroit.	Kahlo miscarries her second child.	Kahlo's mother dies on 15 September.

Self-Portrait on the Borderline Between Mexico and the United States, 1932

oil on metal 31 x 35 cm Collection Manuel Reyero, New York

Diego Rivera thought that the skyscrapers of the United States were objects as fine as the ruins of the ancient civilisations of Mexico, but Kahlo disagreed. Kahlo painted the skyscrapers of America as thin, blank columns reaching into a polluted sky, while the ruins of ancient Mexico sit on fertile ground out of which grows beautiful flowers and life-giving vegetables.

'Dressed in native costume even to huaraches [sandals] she causes much excitement on the streets of San Francisco. People stop in their tracks to look in wonder.'

Photographer Edward Weston (1886-1958) talking about Frida Kahlo

New York

THE GREAT DEPRESSION

Kahlo and Rivera lived in the United States at the time of the Great Depression. In October 1929 US share prices suddenly fell, making many people's savings worthless overnight. Families and companies were ruined and the economic crisis spread to many other countries. Before long, nearly half the banks in America were bankrupt.

In 1932 Franklin Roosevelt (1882-1945) became president. He launched the New Deal, a policy which aimed to help the poorest people and to boost the economy by funding new buildings and public works of art. This created some jobs, but the Depression did not end until 1939, when World War II broke out and factories needed workers to produce equipment for the war.

Kahlo had a love-hate relationship with the United States. On one hand she found Americans unrefined; she hated the huge gap she witnessed between the rich and the poor, she was homesick for Mexico and longed to return. On the other hand she appreciated the differences between Mexico and the United States, saying: '… it did make sense to come here, because it opened my eyes and I have seen an enormous number of new and beautiful things'.

◀ Diego Rivera working on the Rockefeller Center mural he was commissioned to paint in New York, March 1933.

Rivera loved America. He found the country's new machines and multiple cultures inspiring and he continued to accept new commissions. These took the couple from San Francisco to New York and Detroit.

Kahlo and Rivera eventually spent three years in the United States before returning to their new home in San Angel, Mexico City, in December 1933.

◀ People queue to receive free soup and bread because they cannot afford to buy food. Queues like these were common during the Great Depression when more than a quarter of all Americans lost their jobs.

TIMELINE ▶

30 January 1933	March 1933	December 1933
The National Socialists, known as the Nazis, come to power in Germany.	Rivera and Kahlo move to New York so Rivera can paint the mural, *Man at the Crossroads*, at the Rockefeller Center (above).	Kahlo and Rivera return to Mexico.

My Dress Hangs There or New York, 1933

oil and collage on masonite 46 x 50 cm Hoover Gallery, San Francisco

You can tell that Kahlo wanted to return to Mexico when you look at the images in this picture. The streets are covered with pictures, cut out of newspapers, showing people in food queues. A building is on fire on the left, and on the right there is a bin overflowing with rubbish. Kahlo's Mexican costume hangs in New York, but she is not in it – her body and soul are in Mexico. Kahlo also makes fun of the American obssession with sport by placing a trophy on top of one of the two columns in the foreground. The other column has a toilet on it.

'High society here turns me off and I feel a bit of rage against all these rich guys here, since I have seen thousands of people in the most terrible misery without anything to eat and with no place to sleep...'

Frida Kahlo

What is Communism?

Communism is a set of beliefs which centre on the idea that the wealth and property of any country or state should be equally owned by all the people. These ideas were first written about by the Greek philosopher Plato (427-347 BC), but Communism is usually associated with the writings of Karl Marx (1818-83).

Marx was a German philosopher, economist and political thinker who set out his Communist theories in two books: *The Communist Manifesto* (1848), co-written with Friedrich Engels (1920-95), and *Das Kapital* (1867).

▲ Karl Marx lived in London from 1849 until his death in 1883. Until 1864 he was very poor and he and his family lived mostly on bread and potatoes, moving from house to house to avoid debt collectors.

Marx wrote that the history of the world was the history of money and the ownership of money (which was restricted to very few people). Marx called this system capitalism and he felt it was doomed because ordinary working people were bound to rise up – to revolt – and take control of their own futures.

Communism also refers to the political movement which began after World War I (1914-18) and aimed to create entire countries run along Communist lines. The movement set up Communist Parties in many countries and put up candidates for election.

'I only want three things in life: to live with Diego, to continue painting, and to belong to the Communist Party.'

Frida Kahlo

▶ A young boy in a glass factory in Mexico City, c.1930. The Communist Party hoped to encourage workers to take control of factories like this one.

These activists hoped to encourage the working classes to rise up against factory owners and seize power. The first country to become Communist was Russia. It became the Union of Soviet Socialist Republics (or USSR) from 1922 until 1991, when the union broke apart.

▲ A banner made for a Mexican Communist Party march. It shows Josef Stalin (1870-1953), leader of the USSR between 1924 and 1953.

COMMUNISM IN MEXICO

In early 20th-century Mexico there was a great divide between rich and poor. The major industries and land were owned by a tiny number of people, so the majority had no land and no job security. Large numbers of Mexican peasants had very little money, few possessions, and did not own their homes. There was no welfare system to help people when work was scarce, so many almost starved at times.

Communism – with its belief in the equal distribution of wealth – seemed to some Mexicans, including Kahlo and Rivera, the only way to solve the country's social problems.

▲ Kahlo meets Leon Trotsky and his wife (standing on either side of Kahlo) after their arrival in Mexico in 1937.

LEON TROTSKY

Leon Trotsky (1879-1940) was one of the leaders of the Russian Revolution, which led to the founding of the USSR. But Trotsky later clashed with his rival Josef Stalin, who became ruler of the USSR in 1924. In 1929 Trotsky was expelled from Russia. He lived in several European countries, but was constantly under threat from Stalin's agents, who tried to kill him. Rivera helped persuade the Mexican government to offer Trotsky refuge, and on 9 January 1937 Trotsky arrived there with his wife Natalia. They were met by Kahlo on Rivera's behalf and went to stay in her parents' home, the Blue House.

Betrayal

RETABLOS

A *retablo* is a small painting celebrating someone's survival of a misfortune, such as an accident. Each painting has a dedication to God, a saint, or the Virgin Mary in thanks for deliverance from danger. Retablos are also called votive paintings and they are very common in Mexico. They are often painted on metal.

In keeping with this folk art tradition Kahlo started painting on metal in the 1930s (the painting opposite is on sheet metal). She took inspiration from retablos, reproducing their primitive perspectives, limited colour schemes and dedications.

▲ Mexican architect Juan O'Gorman built two separate houses for Rivera and Kahlo, which he linked by a roof-top bridge. Rivera's house (on the left) was pale pink and Kahlo's cobalt blue in colour.

▲ Retablos are still sold from roadside stalls on street corners and outside churches in Mexico today.

When Kahlo returned to Mexico from the United States, she was eager to paint as much as possible. However, there were unhappy times ahead. In 1934 she suffered her third miscarriage and she also discovered that Rivera was having an affair with her sister Cristina.

Devastated, Kahlo left the couple's house in San Angel and moved into an apartment by herself. To show how sad she was Kahlo cut off her long hair (see opposite).

A BROKEN HEART

Memory or *The Heart* shows us how Kahlo felt after discovering Rivera's affair. Her heart has been cut out of her chest and lies on the ground bleeding. It is huge in comparison to her body, symbolising the amount of pain she is suffering.

In December 1935, Kahlo moved back in with Rivera but their marriage was at an end.

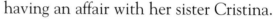

TIMELINE ▶

1934	December 1935	1936	1936-37	9 January 1937
Kahlo's third pregnancy ends after three months. Some toes on her right foot are amputated to relieve her pain. Kahlo discovers Rivera's affair and leaves home.	Kahlo returns to Rivera.	Civil War breaks out in Spain.	Leon Trotsky is given asylum in Mexico.	Trotsky and his wife, Natalia Sedova, arrive in Mexico and move into the Blue House, where they stay until April 1939.

Memory or **The Heart, 1937**
oil on metal 40 x 28 cm Michel Petitjean Collection, Paris
Kahlo portrays herself without hands and floating in thin
air, connected to her clothes by threads, showing that she
feels powerless to change events.

*'I am in such a state
of sadness.'*
Frida Kahlo

Kahlo the Surrealist?

▲ *The Persistence of Memory,*
painted by Salvador Dalí in 1931.

Rivera and Kahlo's relationship continued to deteriorate, but Kahlo began to find success as an artist. In 1938 the French Surrealist poet André Breton (1896-1966) arrived in Mexico to give a series of lectures. Breton decided that Kahlo was a great, undiscovered Surrealist, saying: 'The art of Frida Kahlo is a ribbon around a bomb.'

PAINTING DREAMS

Kahlo responded to Breton's views, explaining: 'I never knew I was a Surrealist until André Breton came to Mexico and told me I was.' She always refused to be associated with any particular artistic movement. Despite Kahlo's protests, her art is sometimes associated with Surrealism – probably because, like Surrealist art, her pictures have a dream-like atmosphere. But Surrealist artists tried to paint the hidden world of people's dreams, whereas Kahlo's pictures are astonishingly aware of her own waking thoughts and feelings.

SURREALISM

Surrealism was a movement founded by André Breton in Paris in 1924. The movement tried to reveal the world of our sleeping minds (called the unconscious) through painting and sculpture, often producing bizarre results. Two of the most famous Surrealist artists are Max Ernst (1891-1976) and Salvador Dalí (1904-89). Ernst used techniques such as 'frottage' (rubbing), which avoided traditional painting and used patterns from rubbings to trigger the imagination. Dalí painted in extreme detail to create a 'real' version of a dream world.

SOLO EXHIBITION

In October 1938 Kahlo travelled alone to New York to prepare for her solo exhibition at the Julien Levy gallery. She exhibited 25 works and her show was considered a success.

▶ **André Breton (on the right) with poet Benjamin Peret and a friend at a Surrealism exhibition.**

TIMELINE ▶

April 1938	October 1938	1938-9
André Breton arrives in Mexico.	Kahlo travels to New York for her solo exhibition at Julien Levy's gallery.	The German army occupies Austria.

The Frame, 1938

oil on aluminium and glass 29 x 22 cm Musée Nationale d'Art Moderne, Paris

This self-portrait was painted on an aluminium sheet, but the frame of the title – the border of
flowers with two birds – was painted on glass which was placed on top of the metal. This painting
was the first 20th-century work by a Mexican artist to be bought by the prestigious Louvre Museum in Paris.

Divorce

KAHLO'S CLOTHES

Kahlo wore Mexican folk costume (as in *The Two Fridas* opposite) because she felt that it brought her closer to the ordinary people of Mexico. Kahlo particularly liked Tehuana clothes, the costume of women from the Isthmus of Tehuantepec. This was usually a long velvet skirt and a white embroidered shirt accompanied by pre-Columbian or colonial jewellery.

▲ Kahlo photographed in New York, 1938-39, in Mexican costume, with her hair traditionally arranged.

In January 1939 Kahlo sailed to Paris to see the work of the Surrealists and to take part in an exhibition called 'Mexique', organised by André Breton. The exhibition included 17 of her paintings, shown alongside documentary photographs as well as pre-Columbian sculptures and popular objects from Mexico. The exhibition was not a great success as Europe was preparing for war with Germany and people were not in the mood to buy pictures.

On Kahlo's return to Mexico it was obvious that her marriage to Rivera was over and she moved into her parents' home, the Blue House. Kahlo and Rivera were divorced on 6 November 1939.

▲ The Surrealists were very interested in pre-Columbian sculpture such as this.

REJECTION BY RIVERA

Kahlo finished *The Two Fridas* on the day her final divorce papers came through, and the picture is filled with the pain she felt at the separation from Rivera. Kahlo has painted two versions of herself – one Frida, in a white dress, is the one Rivera loved; the other, on the right, dressed in simple Tehuana dress (see panel), is the Frida he no longer loves.

The two Fridas hold hands and are also connected by an artery that flows between their two hearts, shown outside their bodies as in *Memory* (see page 27). The Frida in the white dress holds the bleeding end, but because their hearts are connected, the painting suggests both will eventually die.

TIMELINE ▶

Early 1939	March 1939	25 March 1939	September 1939	6 November 1939
The Spanish Civil War ends with the Nationalists taking power.	Kahlo goes to Paris for the 'Mexique' exhibition. Seventeen of her works are shown. Kahlo's self-portrait *The Frame* is bought by the Louvre Museum in Paris.	Kahlo sails for New York. From there she returns to Mexico.	World War II begins in Europe.	Kahlo and Rivera are divorced.

The Two Fridas, 1939
oil on canvas 170 x 170 cm Collection of the Museum of Modern Art, Mexico City
**The Frida on the right-hand side of the picture holds a small portrait of Diego Rivera as a child.
Kahlo included Rivera in her picture because she wanted the viewer to be in no doubt about
who was causing her so much pain. This portrait is now in the Frida Kahlo Museum in Mexico City.**

*'In another period I dressed like a boy with shaved hair,
pants, boots and a leather jacket. But when
I went to see Diego I put on Tehuana costume.'*

Frida Kahlo

Remarriage

In September 1940 Kahlo went to San Francisco for medical treatment. While she was there she met Rivera, who was painting in the city. In December Rivera asked Kahlo to marry him again because, he said, 'Our separation was having a bad effect on both of us.' Kahlo agreed and they were remarried in San Francisco.

A CHANGED WOMAN

In *Self-Portrait with Braid*, painted shortly after Kahlo and Rivera's second marriage, Kahlo expresses her feelings about returning to Rivera. She is surrounded by a plant with jagged and sharp leaves. The stem of the plant seems to reach over her shoulder like a rope keeping her in one position.

The necklace she is wearing looks more like a chain than a piece of jewellery (also see photograph below).

Kahlo knows that the second time around things have changed – she is going into the marriage with her eyes open, no longer Rivera's shy, retiring girl. Now she is an independent woman as well as a recognised artist who can support herself.

▲ Diego Rivera and Frida Kahlo remarried in San Francisco in 1940. Here they are signing the documents that made their marriage legal.

KAHLO'S HAIR

Just as Kahlo wore Tehuana costume to celebrate her Mexican identity (see page 30), she also grew her hair long and arranged it in traditional Mexican styles. Rivera loved her long hair. When Kahlo and Rivera split up in 1934, and again when they divorced in 1939, Kahlo cut her hair short. She wanted to show how desperate she felt at being rejected (you can see her short hair in *Memory* or *The Heart* on page 27).

TIMELINE ▶

17 January 1940	September 1940	8 December 1940	February 1941	14 April 1941
The International Exhibition of Surrealism opens in Mexico City. André Breton is one of the organisers. Kahlo shows one of her works.	Kahlo goes to San Francisco for medical treatment.	Kahlo and Rivera remarry in San Francisco.	Kahlo and Rivera make the Blue House in Coyoacán their home.	Kahlo's father, Guillermo, dies after a heart attack.

Self-Portrait with Braid, 1941

oil on masonite 51 x 38.5 cm Jacques and Natasha Gelman Collection, Mexico City

In this picture Kahlo's hair is long once more and is twisted up into an elaborate traditional design woven with red wool. Kahlo is no longer deserted by love, but her hair looks tight and uncomfortable, more of a burden than a decoration.

Recognition

KAHLO THE TEACHER

Despite her ill health, from 1943 onwards Kahlo taught 12 painting classes a week to students aged between 14 and 19. She enjoyed taking her pupils out of the classroom to find inspiration in the bustling streets of Mexico City. She also encouraged them to read poets such as Walt Whitman (1818-92) and to study nature and biology. She helped her students to absorb the past through art history, sketching pre-Columbian sculptures and visiting Mexico's exotic temples, colonial buildings and beautiful Catholic churches (below).

▶ Rivera reads a letter while Kahlo works in her studio. Their second marriage was a little more peaceful than their first. In the background *The Two Fridas* hangs on the wall, a powerful reminder of past sadness.

Professionally the 1940s were a good time for Kahlo. She took part in group exhibitions and became a member of the Seminario de Cultura Mexicana. This was a government organisation of 25 artists, writers and intellectuals who promoted Mexican art and culture. Kahlo was also interviewed by magazines, and took a teaching job at the School of Painting and Sculpture, Mexico's most famous art school.

STILL LIFES

During the 1940s Kahlo started to create still life paintings – paintings of arranged objects – rather than portraits. As her health worsened she painted more still lifes, such as *The Bride Frightened at Seeing Life Opened* (opposite), than self-portraits. She was often too ill to get out of bed, so it was practical to paint objects which could be arranged in front of her and didn't move.

▲ A 19th-century photograph of the cathedral in Mexico City.

TIMELINE ▶

December 1941	1942	1943
The United States enters World War II. The Mexican economy booms as a result.	Kahlo begins a diary. She is invited to become a member of the Seminario de Cultura Mexicana.	Kahlo becomes a teacher at the School of Painting and Sculpture. She teaches 12 painting classes a week.

La novia que se espanta de ver la vida abierta.

The Bride Frightened at Seeing Life Opened, 1943

oil on canvas 63 x 81.5 cm Jacques and Natasha Gelman Collection, Mexico City

The 'bride' in the picture is the little blonde-haired doll wearing a white dress which pops up over the watermelon in the top left-hand corner of the painting. Kahlo bought this doll in a market on her trip to Paris in 1939. Some people think that Kahlo's still life paintings are self-portraits in a different form. She painted fruits which were bruised and damaged, for example, in place of her own damaged body.

'The only help she gave us was to stimulate us, nothing more. She did not say even half a word about how we should paint, or anything about style… What she taught us, fundamentally, was love of the people, and a taste for "popular" art.'

Arturio Garcia Bustos, one of Frida Kahlo's pupils

Declining health

From 1943 onwards Kahlo spent more time at the Blue House in Coyoacán – she even had to teach from home as she was too frail to travel into the school. Her back and right foot became more and more painful. Kahlo sought comfort in her paintings, her garden and her pets.

CHILDLESS AND LONELY

In *Self-Portrait with Small Monkey* Kahlo expresses her continuing regret at not being able to have children, and her loneliness. Her pet monkey seems to have become her substitute child. The monkey has placed its arm around Kahlo's neck and across her chest, guarding her against further pain and treating her as a trusted friend. Its gaze is as strong and direct as Kahlo's and the monkey stares intelligently out of the canvas. It wears a bow in its hair, which is less elaborate than the one Kahlo wears but is the same colour, making them seem part of the same family.

▲ Rivera and Kahlo with a pet monkey. The couple kept many pets, including small Mexican dogs, parrots, cats, an eagle and a deer.

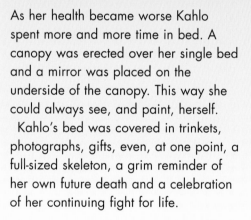

KAHLO'S BED

As her health became worse Kahlo spent more and more time in bed. A canopy was erected over her single bed and a mirror was placed on the underside of the canopy. This way she could always see, and paint, herself.

Kahlo's bed was covered in trinkets, photographs, gifts, even, at one point, a full-sized skeleton, a grim reminder of her own future death and a celebration of her continuing fight for life.

◀ Kahlo's bedroom in the Blue House with trinkets and a mirror fixed above the bed.

TIMELINE ▶

1944	May 1945	July 1945	1946	May 1946	October 1946	1948
Kahlo's health becomes worse and she teaches less and less.	World War II ends in Europe.	Japan surrenders.	Kahlo wins a prize for her painting *Moses*.	Kahlo travels to New York for an operation on her spine.	Kahlo returns to the Blue House.	Kahlo rejoins the Mexican Communist Party.

Self-Portrait with Small Monkey, 1945
oil on masonite 57 x 42 cm Museum Robert Brady, Cuernavaca, Mexico

Kahlo painted several self-portraits which included her pets, but her monkeys appear more often than any other animal. Kahlo's pet monkeys were like children to her and her love of them is obvious, as she always paints them close to her head with their arms around her. But Kahlo's monkeys can also look disturbing because they are wild animals, not children.

Final months

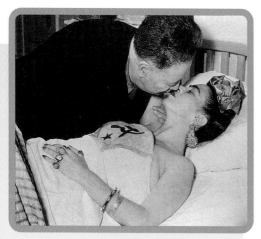

▲ Rivera greets Kahlo in her hospital bed in Mexico City, 1950. Kahlo painted the hammer and sickle – an international sign for Communism – on her plaster corset.

KAHLO'S SPINE

Between 1944 and her death in 1954 Frida Kahlo had worn 28 different medical corsets made of various materials, such as plaster, leather or steel, to give her spine support.

In an attempt to straighten and strengthen her spine she once spent 12 weeks sitting upright in a corset with sandbags on her feet. Another treatment involved Kahlo hanging by her hands from steel rings attached to the ceiling of her hospital room for hours on end to try to stop the vertebrae in her spine from fusing.

In April 1953 Kahlo's first solo exhibition in Mexico opened at the Galeria Arte Contemporaneo in Mexico City. But she was so ill that she was taken to the opening in an ambulance and placed in a four-poster bed when she arrived. In this way Kahlo and her bed became part of the exhibition.

Kahlo's health continued to worsen. In August 1953 her right leg was amputated below the knee and from then on she had to wear an artificial leg.

COMMUNISM

During the last years of her life Kahlo became involved with Communism again. In *Marxism Will Give Health to the Sick*, Kahlo is dressed in a surgical corset, her crutches discarded, thanks to the supporting hands of Communism. But Kahlo was by now very ill – she took drugs to dull the pain she was suffering and had to be tied into her wheelchair to paint.

LAST DAYS

On 2 July 1954, against the advice of her doctors, Kahlo attended a Communist demonstration and was pushed in her wheelchair through the streets of Mexico City. This was her final public appearance – she died two weeks later, weakened by a lifetime of ill health. Her body lay in state in the Palace of Fine Arts in Mexico City. Five hundred people walked behind Frida Kahlo's coffin on its journey to her grave. Diego Rivera was devastated.

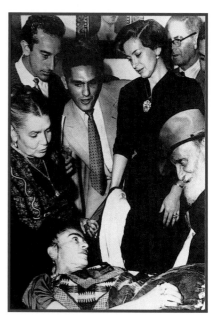

▲ Kahlo at the opening of her only solo exhibition in Mexico. She was so ill that she was unable to speak.

TIMELINE ▶

1950	1951	April 1953	August 1953	July 1954	13 July 1954
Kahlo spends nine months in hospital and endures seven operations.	Kahlo spends most of her time in a wheelchair.	Kahlo's first solo exhibition in Mexico.	Kahlo's right leg is amputated below the knee.	Kahlo catches pneumonia and defies her doctor's orders to go on a demonstration.	Frida Kahlo dies at the age of 47.

Marxism Will Give Health to the Sick, 1954

oil on masonite 76 x 61 cm Frida Kahlo Museum, Mexico City

This picture features a portrait of Karl Marx (see page 24) and a hand strangling Uncle Sam, who symbolises the United States of America. Kahlo was angry at America's development of nuclear weapons (see the mushroom on the right). The dove of peace hovers to the left of the two men.

'In spite of my long illness, I feel immense joy in LIVING.'

Frida Kahlo

Kahlo's legacy

During her lifetime Frida Kahlo was famous for many things – for being Diego Rivera's wife, for her political views, for her physical suffering, for her teaching, for her painting, for her sense of humour, for her love of life. But Kahlo's fame was almost completely confined to Mexico, the country she loved so much.

By the time she died Kahlo had come to be seen as much more than an artist. For many ordinary Mexicans Kahlo's suffering and art had

'Neither… I, nor you, are capable of painting a head like those of Frida Kahlo.'

Pablo Picasso (1881-1973), in a letter to Diego Rivera.

come to symbolise Mexico's struggle against violence and the country's search for its own identity. Mexicans today still call Frida Kahlo 'the soul of Mexico'.

GROWING FAME

Since her death Kahlo's fame, and art, has spread worldwide. Her diary has been translated into many languages. People around the world have read her life story and seen her work in museums and galleries or reproduced in books, posters and cards.

There are Frida Kahlo T-shirts and cookbooks, as well as cosmetics and jewellery inspired by her – and a film has been made of her life, called *Frida*.

▲ On these last two pages of Kahlo's diary the heavens seem to be opening up and crying. On the right an angel with green wings, red hair and heavy black boots looks menacing rather than comforting.

▲ Kahlo's coffin, covered with a Communist flag, is carried down the steps of the Palace of Fine Arts in Mexico City. Diego Rivera is at the front on the right.

FORGING A PATH

During the 1970s, art historians, gallery owners and artists began to study Kahlo's work, and her reputation as an artist has grown ever since. She is now one of the most sought-after painters in the world and is an inspiration to artists everywhere. Works that Kahlo originally gave away as gifts or sold for a few hundred dollars are now fetching huge sums of money.

In November 2000 a tiny painting by Kahlo, only 5 cm high (no bigger than a playing card) was bought for US $400,000, and in 1999 one of her full-size pictures was sold for more than US $10 million.

▲ The Frida Kahlo Museum in Mexico City.

THE FRIDA KAHLO MUSEUM

Frida Kahlo was born in the same house in which she died, at 126 Avenida Londres, Mexico City. It was known as the Blue House, her family home. On 24 November 1957, Diego Rivera died at the age of 70. In his will he left instructions that the Blue House was to be preserved as it was on the day that Kahlo died, and that it be opened to the public as the Frida Kahlo Museum.

On 30 July 1958 the Frida Kahlo Museum opened its doors for the first time and since then hundreds of thousands of people have seen the studio where Kahlo painted, the bed she slept in and her collection of pre-Columbian artefacts and art.

The husband and wife team

Frida Kahlo and Diego Rivera influenced each other's art greatly. Rivera was proud of his wife's work and talked about her to everyone he met. Kahlo was also proud of Rivera's art and would boast of the brilliance of his murals. Rivera encouraged Kahlo to continue painting after her accident and later helped her to find people interested in buying her work. Kahlo advised Rivera on his paintings and gently criticised when she thought a composition, colour or feature was wrong.

DIFFERENT SUBJECTS

Frida Kahlo and Diego Rivera are considered two of the most important artists of modern Mexico, and yet the subjects of their paintings and their styles of painting are very different.

Rivera's paintings are based on grand themes, such as the history of Mexico, but his pictures always include ordinary people. Rivera painted the workers, farmers and small traders of Mexico playing their part in the dramatic history of their country.

'From that time, my obsession was to begin again, painting things just as I saw them with my own eyes and nothing more… Thus, as the accident changed my path, many things prevented me from fulfilling the desires which everyone considers normal, and to me nothing seemed more normal than to paint what had not been fulfilled.'

▲ Frida Kahlo, after her accident in 1925.

'In everything I saw a potential masterpiece – the crowds, the markets, the festivals, the marching battalions, the working men in the shops and fields – in every glowing face, in every luminous child.'

▲ Diego Rivera in his autobiography, *My Art, My Life*.

TIMELINE ▶

1907	1925	1929	1931	1934
1907 Frida Kahlo is born on 6 July in Mexico City.	**1925** Kahlo is seriously injured in a bus accident. She takes months to recover and does not return to school. She starts to paint.	**1929** Kahlo marries Rivera on 21 August. She resigns from the Communist Party after Rivera is expelled. In October the New York Stock Exchange crashes. The Great Depression begins.	**1931** Kahlo returns to Mexico, then goes to New York for a retrospective of Rivera's work.	**1934** Kahlo's third pregnancy ends in miscarriage. Some of her toes are amputated to relieve her pain. She leaves home after discovering Rivera's affair with her sister Cristina.
1910 The Mexican Revolution begins.			**1932** Kahlo travels to New York and Detroit. She miscarries her second child. Her mother dies.	
1913 Polio deforms Kahlo's lower right leg and foot.	**1926** Kahlo is ill again. She wears a plaster corset in bed for four months.	**1930** Kahlo's first pregnancy ends. She moves to San Francisco where Rivera paints murals.		**1935** Kahlo returns home.
1922 Kahlo goes to the Escuela Nacional Preparatoria. She decides to be a doctor. She meets Diego Rivera when he paints a mural at her school.	**1928** Kahlo joins the Mexican Communist Party. She meets Diego Rivera again.		**1933** Rivera paints a mural at the Rockefeller Center, New York. Kahlo and Rivera return to Mexico later that year.	**1937** Leon Trotsky is given asylum in Mexico.

1938 Kahlo travels to New York for a solo exhibition. |

DIFFERENT AIMS

It wasn't just the subject matter of Kahlo's and Rivera's work that was different – the aims of their art were almost completely opposite.

Kahlo's aim was to explore herself through painting.

'…until now, I have managed simply an honest expression of my own self…'

▲ Frida Kahlo talking about her art.

By contrast, Rivera had both a political and a social purpose when he painted. He wanted to offer the poor people of Mexico the hope of a better future through painting a vision of a fairer society.

▶ Diego Rivera in his autobiography, *My Art, My Life.*

▲ Frida Kahlo and Diega Rivera, in a portrait taken in 1939.

'It was my desire to reproduce the pure, basic images of my land. I wanted my paintings to reflect the social life of Mexico as I saw it, and through my vision of the truth, to show the masses the outline of the future.'

1939	1940	1942	1948	1953
1939 Kahlo has 17 works in the 'Mexique' exhibition in Paris. *The Frame* is bought by the Louvre Museum. Kahlo sails for New York, then returns to Mexico. She is divorced from Rivera in November. **September 1939** World War II begins in Europe.	**1940** Kahlo shows a work at the International Exhibition of Surrealism in Mexico City. She goes to San Francisco for medical treatment. She remarries Rivera there. **1941** Kahlo's father dies. **December 1941** The United States enters World War II. The Mexican economy booms as a result.	**1942** Kahlo begins a diary. She joins the Seminario de Cultura Mexicana. **1943** Kahlo teaches painting classes at the School of Painting and Sculpture in Mexico City. **1944** Kahlo's health worsens – she teaches less and less. **May 1945** World War II ends in Europe.	**1946** Kahlo wins a prize for her painting *Moses*. She travels to New York for a spine operation. **1948** Kahlo rejoins the Communist Party. **1950** Kahlo has seven operations and spends nine months in hospital. **1951** Kahlo spends most of her time in a wheelchair.	**1953** Kahlo has her first solo exhibition in Mexico. Her right leg is amputated below the knee. **1954** Kahlo catches pneumonia but defies doctor's orders and goes on a Communist demonstration. She dies on 13 July at the age of 47.

Glossary

artefact: any man-made object of historical importance, such as pottery, jewellery or textiles.

Aztecs: the people who ruled (what is now known as) Central Mexico. The Aztecs defeated the Toltecs in the mid-12th century and were almost wiped out by the Spanish explorer-soldier Hernán Cortés, who arrived in April 1519.

campaign: a plan of action involving marches, speeches, rallies or meetings, designed to educate people about an issue or to achieve a political point.

colonial: from the sixteenth century onwards some European nations, such as Spain, Italy, Portugal, France, Germany and Great Britain, ruled other countries, often by force. This policy was called colonisation. Anything relating to the colonisation of a country can be called colonial, for example a European-style building built by the Spanish in Mexico.

constitution: in politics, the name of the laws, guidelines and rules that dictate the way a country is governed.

coup: the name given to a sudden military attack on the government of a country that brings about a change in political power.

flamboyant: an object that is richly decorated, brilliant or elaborate. A person who creates a commotion or draws attention to themselves by their behaviour.

folk art: the traditional art of a particular people.

folk costume: the traditional style of clothes worn by a people.

frottage: a technique which involves placing a sheet of paper over a textured surface. The paper is rubbed with a pencil. The pattern appears on the paper and can be used to 'trigger' the imagination.

landscape: a painting of scenery.

left-wing: anything relating to the politics of the Left. Communism is the most extreme version of left-wing politics.

Mayans: the Mayan people ruled Mexico between AD 700 and 900. The Mayan culture was very advanced – particularly in astronomy (the study of the stars), mathematics, and writing.

mural: a large painting on a wall.

nationalist: someone who believes passionately in the history, traditions, culture and future of their country.

political activists: people who campaign for changes in society by promoting their own political viewpoint.

pre-Columbian: anything which was created or existed before Italian explorer Christopher Columbus (1451-1506) landed in the Americas in October 1492. Columbus named the Americas the New World and claimed them

for the king and queen of Spain, who had paid for his voyage.

retablo (English, retable): a small painting or other image on a screen, usually incorporating religious symbols.

salon: between the 17th and 20th centuries, a gathering of artists, writers or politicians in a person's home was called a salon.

self-portrait: usually a painting, created by the artist in their own image to reflect his or her feelings or state of mind.

still life: a picture of objects that do not move, usually carefully arranged by the artist.

Surrealism: an intellectual movement that emerged in the 1920s that tried to depict the life of our unconscious minds and dreams. The Surrealists included artists, writers and film-makers.

symbols: an object used to represent something which cannot be seen, such as an idea or feeling.

Toltecs: the people who ruled what is now Central Mexico between the 10th and 12th centuries AD. The Toltecs were famed as builders, craftsmen and metalworkers.

unconscious: describes the part of a person's mind that lies outside the conscious mind we use in everyday waking life. Dreams and the imagination are expressions of the unconscious.

Museums and galleries

Works by Kahlo are exhibited in museums and galleries in many parts of the world. Some of those listed here are devoted solely to Kahlo, but most have a wide range of other artists' works on display.

Even if you can't visit any of these galleries yourself, you may be able to visit their websites. Gallery websites often show pictures of the artworks they have on display. Some of the websites even offer virtual tours which allow you to wander around and look at different paintings while sitting comfortably in front of your computer!

Most of the international websites detailed below include an option that allows you to view them in English.

MEXICO

Dolores Almedo Collection
Hacienda La Noria
5843 Avenue Mexico
Xochimilco District
Mexico City
www.mexconnect.com

Frida Kahlo Museum
247 Londres Street
Allende
Coyoacán
Mexico City
You can look at the museum
via www.mexconnect.com

Jacques and Natasha Gelman Collection
Mexico City
This collection has been bequeathed to the Metropolitan Museum of Art, New York

National Museum of Art
Calle Tacuba
Col Centro
Del Cuantamoc
Mexico City 06010

USA

Albright-Knox Art Gallery
1285 Elmwood Avenue
Buffalo
New York
14222-1096
www.albrightknox.org

Harry Ransom Humanities Research Center Art Collection
21st and Guadalupe
PO Box 7249
Austin
Texas 78713-7219
www.hrc.utexas.edu

Metropolitan Museum of Art
100 Fifth Avenue
NY 10028
New York
www.metmuseum.org

Museum of Fine Arts
Avenue of The Arts
465 Huntingdon Avenue
Boston
Massachusetts
02115-5523
www.mfa.org/home.htm

Museum of Modern Art
33 Street at Queens Blvd,
Long Island City,
Queens, New York
www.moma.org

Phoenix Art Museum
1625 North Central Avenue
Phoenix
Arizona
85004-1685
www.phxart.org

San Francisco Museum of Modern Art
151 Third Street
(Between Mission and Howard Street)
San Francisco
CA 94103-3159
www.sfmoma.org

The National Museum for Women in the Arts
1250 New York Avenue NW
Washington DC
20005 3920
www.nmwa.org/

EUROPE

Musée Nationale d'Art Moderne
Centre Georges Pompidou
Place Georges Pompidou
Paris 75004
France
www.centrepompidou.fr

Index